This Planner Belongs to:

_____

_____

_____

2020

January

S	M	T	W	T	F	S
		1	2	3	4	
5	6	7	8	9	10	11
12	13	14	15	16	17	18
19	20	21	22	23	24	25
26	27	28	29	30	31	

February

S	M	T	W	T	F	S
						1
2	3	4	5	6	7	8
9	10	11	12	13	14	15
16	17	18	19	20	21	22
23	24	25	26	27	28	29

March

S	M	T	W	T	F	S
1	2	3	4	5	6	7
8	9	10	11	12	13	14
15	16	17	18	19	20	21
22	23	24	25	26	27	28
29	30	31				

April

S	M	T	W	T	F	S
		1	2	3	4	
5	6	7	8	9	10	11
12	13	14	15	16	17	18
19	20	21	22	23	24	25
26	27	28	29	30		

May

S	M	T	W	T	F	S
					1	2
3	4	5	6	7	8	9
10	11	12	13	14	15	16
17	18	19	20	21	22	23
24	25	26	27	28	29	30
31						

June

S	M	T	W	T	F	S
	1	2	3	4	5	6
7	8	9	10	11	12	13
14	15	16	17	18	19	20
21	22	23	24	25	26	27
28	29	30				

July

S	M	T	W	T	F	S
		1	2	3	4	
5	6	7	8	9	10	11
12	13	14	15	16	17	18
19	20	21	22	23	24	25
26	27	28	29	30	31	

August

S	M	T	W	T	F	S
						1
2	3	4	5	6	7	8
9	10	11	12	13	14	15
16	17	18	19	20	21	22
23	24	25	26	27	28	29
30	31					

September

S	M	T	W	T	F	S
		1	2	3	4	5
6	7	8	9	10	11	12
13	14	15	16	17	18	19
20	21	22	23	24	25	26
27	28	29	30			

October

S	M	T	W	T	F	S
				1	2	3
4	5	6	7	8	9	10
11	12	13	14	15	16	17
18	19	20	21	22	23	24
25	26	27	28	29	30	31

November

S	M	T	W	T	F	S
1	2	3	4	5	6	7
8	9	10	11	12	13	14
15	16	17	18	19	20	21
22	23	24	25	26	27	28
29	30					

December

S	M	T	W	T	F	S
		1	2	3	4	5
6	7	8	9	10	11	12
13	14	15	16	17	18	19
20	21	22	23	24	25	26
27	28	29	30	31		

JANUARY 2020

SUNDAY	MONDAY	TUESDAY	WEDNESDAY
			1
5	6	7	8
12	13	14	15
19	20	21	22
26	27	28	29

THURSDAY	FRIDAY	SATURDAY	NOTES
2	3	4	
9	10	11	
16	17	18	
23	24	25	
30	31		

FEBRUARY 2020

SUNDAY	MONDAY	TUESDAY	WEDNESDAY
2	3	4	5
9	10	11	12
16	17	18	19
23	24	25	26

THURSDAY	FRIDAY	SATURDAY	NOTES
		1	
6	7	8	
13	14	15	
20	21	22	
27	28	29	

MARCH 2020

SUNDAY	MONDAY	TUESDAY	WEDNESDAY
1	2	3	4
8	9	10	11
15	16	17	18
22	23	24	25
29	30	31	

THURSDAY	FRIDAY	SATURDAY	NOTES
5	6	7	
12	13	14	
19	20	21	
26	27	28	

APRIL 2020

SUNDAY	MONDAY	TUESDAY	WEDNESDAY
			1
5	6	7	8
12	13	14	15
19	20	21	22
26	27	28	29

THURSDAY	FRIDAY	SATURDAY	NOTES
2	3	4	
9	10	11	
16	17	18	
23	24	25	
30			

MAY 2020

SUNDAY	MONDAY	TUESDAY	WEDNESDAY
3	4	5	6
10	11	12	13
17	18	19	20
24	25	26	27

THURSDAY	FRIDAY	SATURDAY	NOTES
	1	2	_____ _____ _____ _____ _____
7	8	9	_____ _____ _____ _____
14	15	16	_____ _____ _____ _____ _____
21	22	23	_____ _____ _____ _____
28	29	30	_____ _____ _____ _____

JUNE 2020

SUNDAY	MONDAY	TUESDAY	WEDNESDAY
	1	2	3
7	8	9	10
14	15	16	17
21	22	23	24
28	29	30	

THURSDAY	FRIDAY	SATURDAY	NOTES
4	5	6	
11	12	13	
18	19	20	
25	26	27	

JULY 2020

SUNDAY	MONDAY	TUESDAY	WEDNESDAY
			1
5	6	7	8
12	13	14	15
19	20	21	22
26	27	28	29

THURSDAY	FRIDAY	SATURDAY	NOTES
2	3	4	
9	10	11	
16	17	18	
23	24	25	
30	31		

AUGUST 2020

SUNDAY	MONDAY	TUESDAY	WEDNESDAY
2	3	4	5
9	10	11	12
16	17	18	19
23	24	25	26

THURSDAY	FRIDAY	SATURDAY	NOTES
		1	
6	7	8	
13	14	15	
20	21	22	
27	28	29	

SEPTEMBER 2020

SUNDAY	MONDAY	TUESDAY	WEDNESDAY
		1	2
6	7	8	9
13	14	15	16
20	21	22	23
27	28	29	30

THURSDAY	FRIDAY	SATURDAY	NOTES
3	4	5	
10	11	12	
17	18	19	
24	25	26	

OCTOBER 2020

SUNDAY	MONDAY	TUESDAY	WEDNESDAY
4	5	6	7
11	12	13	14
18	19	20	21
25	26	27	28

THURSDAY	FRIDAY	SATURDAY	NOTES
1	2	3	
8	9	10	
15	16	17	
22	23	24	
29	30	31	

NOVEMBER 2020

SUNDAY	MONDAY	TUESDAY	WEDNESDAY
1	2	3	4
8	9	10	11
15	16	17	18
22	23	24	25
29	30		

THURSDAY	FRIDAY	SATURDAY	NOTES
5	6	7	
12	13	14	
19	20	21	
26	27	28	

DECEMBER 2020

SUNDAY	MONDAY	TUESDAY	WEDNESDAY
		1	2
6	7	8	9
13	14	15	16
20	21	22	23
27	28	29	30

THURSDAY	FRIDAY	SATURDAY	NOTES
3	4	5	
10	11	12	
17	18	19	
24	25	26	
31			

MON • December 30, 2019

_____
_____
_____
_____
_____
_____
_____

○ _____
○ _____
○ _____
○ _____
○ _____
○ _____
○ _____

TUE • December 31, 2019

_____
_____
_____
_____
_____
_____
_____

○ _____
○ _____
○ _____
○ _____
○ _____
○ _____
○ _____

WED • January 01, 2020

_____
_____
_____
_____
_____
_____
_____

○ _____
○ _____
○ _____
○ _____
○ _____
○ _____
○ _____

THU • January 02, 2020

_____
_____
_____
_____
_____
_____
_____

○ _____
○ _____
○ _____
○ _____
○ _____
○ _____
○ _____

F R I • January 03, 2020

_____   ○   _____
_____   ○   _____
_____   ○   _____
_____   ○   _____
_____   ○   _____
_____   ○   _____
_____   ○   _____

S A T • January 04, 2020

_____   ○   _____
_____   ○   _____
_____   ○   _____
_____   ○   _____
_____   ○   _____
_____   ○   _____
_____   ○   _____

S U N • January 05, 2020

_____   ○   _____
_____   ○   _____
_____   ○   _____
_____   ○   _____
_____   ○   _____
_____   ○   _____
_____   ○   _____

NOTES   ## TO DO

_____   ○   _____
_____   ○   _____
_____   ○   _____
_____   ○   _____
_____   ○   _____
_____   ○   _____
_____   ○   _____

MON • January 06, 2020

○
○
○
○
○
○
○
○

TUE • January 07, 2020

○
○
○
○
○
○
○

WED • January 08, 2020

○
○
○
○
○
○
○

THU • January 09, 2020

○
○
○
○
○
○
○

■ F R I • January 10, 2020

_____ ○ _____
_____ ○ _____
_____ ○ _____
_____ ○ _____
_____ ○ _____
_____ ○ _____
_____ ○ _____

■ S A T • January 11, 2020

_____ ○ _____
_____ ○ _____
_____ ○ _____
_____ ○ _____
_____ ○ _____
_____ ○ _____
_____ ○ _____

■ S U N • January 12, 2020

_____ ○ _____
_____ ○ _____
_____ ○ _____
_____ ○ _____
_____ ○ _____
_____ ○ _____
_____ ○ _____

NOTES   ## TO DO

_____ ○ _____
_____ ○ _____
_____ ○ _____
_____ ○ _____
_____ ○ _____
_____ ○ _____
                           ○ _____

MON • January 13, 2020

○
○
○
○
○
○
○

TUE • January 14, 2020

○
○
○
○
○
○
○

WED • January 15, 2020

○
○
○
○
○
○
○

THU • January 16, 2020

○
○
○
○
○
○
○

F R I • January 17, 2020

_____   ○   _____
_____   ○   _____
_____   ○   _____
_____   ○   _____
_____   ○   _____
_____   ○   _____
_____   ○   _____

S A T • January 18, 2020

_____   ○   _____
_____   ○   _____
_____   ○   _____
_____   ○   _____
_____   ○   _____
_____   ○   _____
_____   ○   _____

S U N • January 19, 2020

_____   ○   _____
_____   ○   _____
_____   ○   _____
_____   ○   _____
_____   ○   _____
_____   ○   _____
_____   ○   _____

NOTES

_____
_____
_____
_____
_____

TO DO

○   _____
○   _____
○   _____
○   _____
○   _____
○   _____
○   _____

MON • January 20, 2020

- ○
- ○
- ○
- ○
- ○
- ○
- ○

TUE • January 21, 2020

- ○
- ○
- ○
- ○
- ○
- ○
- ○

WED • January 22, 2020

- ○
- ○
- ○
- ○
- ○
- ○
- ○

THU • January 23, 2020

- ○
- ○
- ○
- ○
- ○
- ○
- ○

F R I • January 24, 2020

○
○
○
○
○
○
○

S A T • January 25, 2020

○
○
○
○
○
○
○

S U N • January 26, 2020

○
○
○
○
○
○
○

NOTES

TO DO

○
○
○
○
○
○
○

■ M O N • January 27, 2020

_____ ○
_____ ○ _____
_____ ○ _____
_____ ○ _____
_____ ○ _____
_____ ○ _____
_____ ○ _____
                         ○ _____

■ T U E • January 28, 2020

_____ ○
_____ ○ _____
_____ ○ _____
_____ ○ _____
_____ ○ _____
_____ ○ _____
_____ ○ _____
                         ○ _____

■ W E D • January 29, 2020

_____ ○
_____ ○ _____
_____ ○ _____
_____ ○ _____
_____ ○ _____
_____ ○ _____
_____ ○ _____
                         ○ _____

■ T H U • January 30, 2020

_____ ○
_____ ○ _____
_____ ○ _____
_____ ○ _____
_____ ○ _____
_____ ○ _____
_____ ○ _____
                         ○ _____

F R I • January 31, 2020

_____   ○
_____   ○ _____
_____   ○ _____
_____   ○ _____
_____   ○ _____
_____   ○ _____
_____   ○ _____
                            ○ _____

S A T • February 01, 2020

_____   ○
_____   ○ _____
_____   ○ _____
_____   ○ _____
_____   ○ _____
_____   ○ _____
_____   ○ _____
                            ○ _____

S U N • February 02, 2020

_____   ○
_____   ○ _____
_____   ○ _____
_____   ○ _____
_____   ○ _____
_____   ○ _____
_____   ○ _____
                            ○ _____

NOTES   ## TO DO

_____   ○
_____   ○ _____
_____   ○ _____
_____   ○ _____
_____   ○ _____
_____   ○ _____
                            ○ _____

M O N • February 03, 2020

_____

T U   E • February 04, 2020

_____

W E D • February 05, 2020

_____

T H   U • February 06, 2020

_____

F R I • February 07, 2020

_____   ○   _____
_____   ○   _____
_____   ○   _____
_____   ○   _____
_____   ○   _____
_____   ○   _____
_____   ○   _____

S A T • February 08, 2020

_____   ○   _____
_____   ○   _____
_____   ○   _____
_____   ○   _____
_____   ○   _____
_____   ○   _____
_____   ○   _____

S U N • February 09, 2020

_____   ○   _____
_____   ○   _____
_____   ○   _____
_____   ○   _____
_____   ○   _____
_____   ○   _____
_____   ○   _____

NOTES   ## TO DO

_____   ○   _____
_____   ○   _____
_____   ○   _____
_____   ○   _____
_____   ○   _____
_____   ○   _____
                        ○   _____

MON • February 10, 2020

- _____ ○ _____
- _____ ○ _____
- _____ ○ _____
- _____ ○ _____
- _____ ○ _____
- _____ ○ _____
- _____ ○ _____
- _____ ○ _____

TUE • February 11, 2020

- _____ ○ _____
- _____ ○ _____
- _____ ○ _____
- _____ ○ _____
- _____ ○ _____
- _____ ○ _____
- _____ ○ _____

WED • February 12, 2020

- _____ ○ _____
- _____ ○ _____
- _____ ○ _____
- _____ ○ _____
- _____ ○ _____
- _____ ○ _____
- _____ ○ _____

THU • February 13, 2020

- _____ ○ _____
- _____ ○ _____
- _____ ○ _____
- _____ ○ _____
- _____ ○ _____
- _____ ○ _____
- _____ ○ _____

F R I • February 14, 2020

_____   ◯ _____
_____   ◯ _____
_____   ◯ _____
_____   ◯ _____
_____   ◯ _____
_____   ◯ _____
_____   ◯ _____

S A T • February 15, 2020

_____   ◯ _____
_____   ◯ _____
_____   ◯ _____
_____   ◯ _____
_____   ◯ _____
_____   ◯ _____
_____   ◯ _____

S U N • February 16, 2020

_____   ◯ _____
_____   ◯ _____
_____   ◯ _____
_____   ◯ _____
_____   ◯ _____
_____   ◯ _____
_____   ◯ _____

NOTES   ## TO DO

_____   ◯ _____
_____   ◯ _____
_____   ◯ _____
_____   ◯ _____
_____   ◯ _____
_____   ◯ _____
                                    ◯ _____

MON • February 17, 2020

- ○
- ○
- ○
- ○
- ○
- ○
- ○

TUE • February 18, 2020

- ○
- ○
- ○
- ○
- ○
- ○
- ○

WED • February 19, 2020

- ○
- ○
- ○
- ○
- ○
- ○
- ○

THU • February 20, 2020

- ○
- ○
- ○
- ○
- ○
- ○
- ○

■ F R I • February 21, 2020

_____   ○ _____
_____   ○ _____
_____   ○ _____
_____   ○ _____
_____   ○ _____
_____   ○ _____
_____   ○ _____

■ S A T • February 22, 2020

_____   ○ _____
_____   ○ _____
_____   ○ _____
_____   ○ _____
_____   ○ _____
_____   ○ _____
_____   ○ _____

■ S U N • February 23, 2020

_____   ○ _____
_____   ○ _____
_____   ○ _____
_____   ○ _____
_____   ○ _____
_____   ○ _____
_____   ○ _____

NOTES   ## TO DO

_____   ○ _____
_____   ○ _____
_____   ○ _____
_____   ○ _____
_____   ○ _____
_____   ○ _____
                                     ○ _____

MON • February 24, 2020

TUE • February 25, 2020

WED • February 26, 2020

THU • February 27, 2020

F R I • February 28, 2020

_____ ○ _____
_____ ○ _____
_____ ○ _____
_____ ○ _____
_____ ○ _____
_____ ○ _____
_____ ○ _____

S A T • February 29, 2020

_____ ○ _____
_____ ○ _____
_____ ○ _____
_____ ○ _____
_____ ○ _____
_____ ○ _____
_____ ○ _____

S U N • March 01, 2020

_____ ○ _____
_____ ○ _____
_____ ○ _____
_____ ○ _____
_____ ○ _____
_____ ○ _____
_____ ○ _____

NOTES   ## TO DO

_____ ○ _____
_____ ○ _____
_____ ○ _____
_____ ○ _____
_____ ○ _____
_____ ○ _____
                       ○ _____

MON • March 02, 2020

_____ ○
_____ ○ _____
_____ ○ _____
_____ ○ _____
_____ ○ _____
_____ ○ _____
_____ ○ _____
                          ○ _____

TUE • March 03, 2020

_____ ○
_____ ○ _____
_____ ○ _____
_____ ○ _____
_____ ○ _____
_____ ○ _____
_____ ○ _____
                          ○ _____

WED • March 04, 2020

_____ ○
_____ ○ _____
_____ ○ _____
_____ ○ _____
_____ ○ _____
_____ ○ _____
_____ ○ _____
                          ○ _____

THU • March 05, 2020

_____ ○
_____ ○ _____
_____ ○ _____
_____ ○ _____
_____ ○ _____
_____ ○ _____
_____ ○ _____
                          ○ _____

F R I • March 06, 2020

_____   ○   _____
_____   ○   _____
_____   ○   _____
_____   ○   _____
_____   ○   _____
_____   ○   _____
_____   ○   _____

S A T • March 07, 2020

_____   ○   _____
_____   ○   _____
_____   ○   _____
_____   ○   _____
_____   ○   _____
_____   ○   _____
_____   ○   _____

S U N • March 08, 2020

_____   ○   _____
_____   ○   _____
_____   ○   _____
_____   ○   _____
_____   ○   _____
_____   ○   _____
_____   ○   _____

NOTES   TO DO

_____   ○   _____
_____   ○   _____
_____   ○   _____
_____   ○   _____
_____   ○   _____
_____   ○   _____
_____   ○   _____

MON • March 09, 2020

○
○
○
○
○
○
○

TUE • March 10, 2020

○
○
○
○
○
○
○

WED • March 11, 2020

○
○
○
○
○
○
○

THU • March 12, 2020

○
○
○
○
○
○
○

FRI • March 13, 2020

_____ ○ _____
_____ ○ _____
_____ ○ _____
_____ ○ _____
_____ ○ _____
_____ ○ _____
_____ ○ _____

SAT • March 14, 2020

_____ ○ _____
_____ ○ _____
_____ ○ _____
_____ ○ _____
_____ ○ _____
_____ ○ _____
_____ ○ _____

SUN • March 15, 2020

_____ ○ _____
_____ ○ _____
_____ ○ _____
_____ ○ _____
_____ ○ _____
_____ ○ _____
_____ ○ _____

NOTES

_____

_____

_____

_____

_____

_____

TO DO

○ _____
○ _____
○ _____
○ _____
○ _____
○ _____
○ _____

MON • March 16, 2020

_____ ○ _____
_____ ○ _____
_____ ○ _____
_____ ○ _____
_____ ○ _____
_____ ○ _____
_____ ○ _____

TUE • March 17, 2020

_____ ○ _____
_____ ○ _____
_____ ○ _____
_____ ○ _____
_____ ○ _____
_____ ○ _____
_____ ○ _____

WED • March 18, 2020

_____ ○ _____
_____ ○ _____
_____ ○ _____
_____ ○ _____
_____ ○ _____
_____ ○ _____
_____ ○ _____

THU • March 19, 2020

_____ ○ _____
_____ ○ _____
_____ ○ _____
_____ ○ _____
_____ ○ _____
_____ ○ _____
_____ ○ _____

F R I • March 20, 2020

_____   ○
_____   ○   _____
_____   ○   _____
_____   ○   _____
_____   ○   _____
_____   ○   _____
_____   ○   _____
_____   ○   _____

S A T • March 21, 2020

_____   ○
_____   ○   _____
_____   ○   _____
_____   ○   _____
_____   ○   _____
_____   ○   _____
_____   ○   _____
_____   ○   _____

S U N • March 22, 2020

_____   ○
_____   ○   _____
_____   ○   _____
_____   ○   _____
_____   ○   _____
_____   ○   _____
_____   ○   _____

NOTES   ## TO DO

_____   ○
_____   ○   _____
_____   ○   _____
_____   ○   _____
_____   ○   _____
_____   ○   _____
_____   ○   _____

MON • March 23, 2020

_____ ○
_____ ○ _____
_____ ○ _____
_____ ○ _____
_____ ○ _____
_____ ○ _____
_____ ○ _____
                         ○ _____

TUE • March 24, 2020

_____ ○
_____ ○ _____
_____ ○ _____
_____ ○ _____
_____ ○ _____
_____ ○ _____
_____ ○ _____
                         ○ _____

WED • March 25, 2020

_____ ○
_____ ○ _____
_____ ○ _____
_____ ○ _____
_____ ○ _____
_____ ○ _____
_____ ○ _____

THU • March 26, 2020

_____ ○
_____ ○ _____
_____ ○ _____
_____ ○ _____
_____ ○ _____
_____ ○ _____
_____ ○ _____

F R I • March 27, 2020

_____   ○ _____
_____   ○ _____
_____   ○ _____
_____   ○ _____
_____   ○ _____
_____   ○ _____
_____   ○ _____
_____   ○ _____

S A T • March 28, 2020

_____   ○ _____
_____   ○ _____
_____   ○ _____
_____   ○ _____
_____   ○ _____
_____   ○ _____
_____   ○ _____

S U N • March 29, 2020

_____   ○ _____
_____   ○ _____
_____   ○ _____
_____   ○ _____
_____   ○ _____
_____   ○ _____
_____   ○ _____

NOTES   ## TO DO

_____   ○ _____
_____   ○ _____
_____   ○ _____
_____   ○ _____
_____   ○ _____
_____   ○ _____
                               ○ _____

MON • March 30, 2020

_____   ○   _____
_____   ○   _____
_____   ○   _____
_____   ○   _____
_____   ○   _____
_____   ○   _____
_____   ○   _____
_____   ○   _____

TUE • March 31, 2020

_____   ○   _____
_____   ○   _____
_____   ○   _____
_____   ○   _____
_____   ○   _____
_____   ○   _____
_____   ○   _____

WED • April 01, 2020

_____   ○   _____
_____   ○   _____
_____   ○   _____
_____   ○   _____
_____   ○   _____
_____   ○   _____
_____   ○   _____

THU • April 02, 2020

_____   ○   _____
_____   ○   _____
_____   ○   _____
_____   ○   _____
_____   ○   _____
_____   ○   _____
_____   ○   _____

F R I • April 03, 2020

_____   ○ _____
_____   ○ _____
_____   ○ _____
_____   ○ _____
_____   ○ _____
_____   ○ _____
_____   ○ _____

S A T • April 04, 2020

_____   ○ _____
_____   ○ _____
_____   ○ _____
_____   ○ _____
_____   ○ _____
_____   ○ _____
_____   ○ _____

S U N • April 05, 2020

_____   ○ _____
_____   ○ _____
_____   ○ _____
_____   ○ _____
_____   ○ _____
_____   ○ _____
_____   ○ _____

NOTES   ## TO DO

_____   ○ _____
_____   ○ _____
_____   ○ _____
_____   ○ _____
_____   ○ _____
_____   ○ _____
_____   ○ _____

MON • April 06, 2020

_____ ○ _____
_____ ○ _____
_____ ○ _____
_____ ○ _____
_____ ○ _____
_____ ○ _____
_____ ○ _____

TUE • April 07, 2020

_____ ○ _____
_____ ○ _____
_____ ○ _____
_____ ○ _____
_____ ○ _____
_____ ○ _____
_____ ○ _____

WED • April 08, 2020

_____ ○ _____
_____ ○ _____
_____ ○ _____
_____ ○ _____
_____ ○ _____
_____ ○ _____
_____ ○ _____

THU • April 09, 2020

_____ ○ _____
_____ ○ _____
_____ ○ _____
_____ ○ _____
_____ ○ _____
_____ ○ _____
_____ ○ _____

F R I • April 10, 2020

_____   ○
_____   ○   _____
_____   ○   _____
_____   ○   _____
_____   ○   _____
_____   ○   _____
_____   ○   _____
                          ○   _____

S A T • April 11, 2020

_____   ○
_____   ○   _____
_____   ○   _____
_____   ○   _____
_____   ○   _____
_____   ○   _____
_____   ○   _____
                          ○   _____

S U N • April 12, 2020

_____   ○
_____   ○   _____
_____   ○   _____
_____   ○   _____
_____   ○   _____
_____   ○   _____
_____   ○   _____
                          ○   _____

NOTES   ## TO DO

_____   ○
_____   ○   _____
_____   ○   _____
_____   ○   _____
_____   ○   _____
_____   ○   _____
                          ○   _____

MON • April 13, 2020

_____
_____   ○
_____   ○
_____   ○
_____   ○
_____   ○
_____   ○
                            ○

TUE • April 14, 2020

_____
_____   ○
_____   ○
_____   ○
_____   ○
_____   ○
_____   ○
                            ○

WED • April 15, 2020

_____
_____   ○
_____   ○
_____   ○
_____   ○
_____   ○
_____   ○
                            ○

THU • April 16, 2020

_____
_____   ○
_____   ○
_____   ○
_____   ○
_____   ○
_____   ○
                            ○

F R I • April 17, 2020

S A T • April 18, 2020

S U N • April 19, 2020

NOTES

TO DO

MON • April 20, 2020

_____ ○
_____ ○ _____
_____ ○ _____
_____ ○ _____
_____ ○ _____
_____ ○ _____
_____ ○ _____
_____   _____

TUE • April 21, 2020

_____ ○
_____ ○ _____
_____ ○ _____
_____ ○ _____
_____ ○ _____
_____ ○ _____
_____ ○ _____
_____   _____

WED • April 22, 2020

_____ ○
_____ ○ _____
_____ ○ _____
_____ ○ _____
_____ ○ _____
_____ ○ _____
_____ ○ _____
_____   _____

THU • April 23, 2020

_____ ○
_____ ○ _____
_____ ○ _____
_____ ○ _____
_____ ○ _____
_____ ○ _____
_____ ○ _____
_____   _____

F R I • April 24, 2020

○
○
○
○
○
○
○

S A T • April 25, 2020

○
○
○
○
○
○
○

S U N • April 26, 2020

○
○
○
○
○
○
○

NOTES

TO DO

○
○
○
○
○
○
○

MON • April 27, 2020

_____ ○ _____
_____ ○ _____
_____ ○ _____
_____ ○ _____
_____ ○ _____
_____ ○ _____
_____ ○ _____

TUE • April 28, 2020

_____ ○ _____
_____ ○ _____
_____ ○ _____
_____ ○ _____
_____ ○ _____
_____ ○ _____
_____ ○ _____

WED • April 29, 2020

_____ ○ _____
_____ ○ _____
_____ ○ _____
_____ ○ _____
_____ ○ _____
_____ ○ _____
_____ ○ _____

THU • April 30, 2020

_____ ○ _____
_____ ○ _____
_____ ○ _____
_____ ○ _____
_____ ○ _____
_____ ○ _____
_____ ○ _____

F R I • May 01, 2020

_____   ◯ _____
_____   ◯ _____
_____   ◯ _____
_____   ◯ _____
_____   ◯ _____
_____   ◯ _____
_____   ◯ _____

S A T • May 02, 2020

_____   ◯ _____
_____   ◯ _____
_____   ◯ _____
_____   ◯ _____
_____   ◯ _____
_____   ◯ _____
_____   ◯ _____

S U N • May 03, 2020

_____   ◯ _____
_____   ◯ _____
_____   ◯ _____
_____   ◯ _____
_____   ◯ _____
_____   ◯ _____
_____   ◯ _____

NOTES

_____
_____
_____
_____
_____

TO DO

◯ _____
◯ _____
◯ _____
◯ _____
◯ _____
◯ _____
◯ _____

■ MON • May 04, 2020

_____ ○ _____
_____ ○ _____
_____ ○ _____
_____ ○ _____
_____ ○ _____
_____ ○ _____
_____ ○ _____

■ TUE • May 05, 2020

_____ ○ _____
_____ ○ _____
_____ ○ _____
_____ ○ _____
_____ ○ _____
_____ ○ _____
_____ ○ _____

■ WED • May 06, 2020

_____ ○ _____
_____ ○ _____
_____ ○ _____
_____ ○ _____
_____ ○ _____
_____ ○ _____
_____ ○ _____

■ THU • May 07, 2020

_____ ○ _____
_____ ○ _____
_____ ○ _____
_____ ○ _____
_____ ○ _____
_____ ○ _____
_____ ○ _____

FRI • May 08, 2020

_____ ◯ _____
_____ ◯ _____
_____ ◯ _____
_____ ◯ _____
_____ ◯ _____
_____ ◯ _____
_____ ◯ _____

SAT • May 09, 2020

_____ ◯ _____
_____ ◯ _____
_____ ◯ _____
_____ ◯ _____
_____ ◯ _____
_____ ◯ _____
_____ ◯ _____

SUN • May 10, 2020

_____ ◯ _____
_____ ◯ _____
_____ ◯ _____
_____ ◯ _____
_____ ◯ _____
_____ ◯ _____
_____ ◯ _____

NOTES

TO DO

_____ ◯ _____
_____ ◯ _____
_____ ◯ _____
_____ ◯ _____
_____ ◯ _____
_____ ◯ _____
_____ ◯ _____

MON • May 11, 2020

_____ ○
_____ ○ _____
_____ ○ _____
_____ ○ _____
_____ ○ _____
_____ ○ _____
_____ ○ _____
                          ○ _____

TUE • May 12, 2020

                          ○
_____ ○ _____
_____ ○ _____
_____ ○ _____
_____ ○ _____
_____ ○ _____
_____ ○ _____
_____ ○ _____

WED • May 13, 2020

                          ○
_____ ○ _____
_____ ○ _____
_____ ○ _____
_____ ○ _____
_____ ○ _____
_____ ○ _____
_____ ○ _____

THU • May 14, 2020

                          ○
_____ ○ _____
_____ ○ _____
_____ ○ _____
_____ ○ _____
_____ ○ _____
_____ ○ _____
                          ○

◼ F R I • May 15, 2020

_____   ◯   _____
_____   ◯   _____
_____   ◯   _____
_____   ◯   _____
_____   ◯   _____
_____   ◯   _____
_____   ◯   _____

◼ S A T • May 16, 2020

_____   ◯   _____
_____   ◯   _____
_____   ◯   _____
_____   ◯   _____
_____   ◯   _____
_____   ◯   _____
_____   ◯   _____

◼ S U N • May 17, 2020

_____   ◯   _____
_____   ◯   _____
_____   ◯   _____
_____   ◯   _____
_____   ◯   _____
_____   ◯   _____
_____   ◯   _____

NOTES   TO DO

_____   ◯   _____
_____   ◯   _____
_____   ◯   _____
_____   ◯   _____
_____   ◯   _____
_____   ◯   _____
_____   ◯   _____

MON • May 18, 2020

_____
_____
_____
_____
_____
_____
_____

○ _____
○ _____
○ _____
○ _____
○ _____
○ _____
○ _____

TUE • May 19, 2020

_____
_____
_____
_____
_____
_____
_____

○ _____
○ _____
○ _____
○ _____
○ _____
○ _____
○ _____

WED • May 20, 2020

_____
_____
_____
_____
_____
_____
_____

○ _____
○ _____
○ _____
○ _____
○ _____
○ _____
○ _____

THU • May 21, 2020

_____
_____
_____
_____
_____
_____

○ _____
○ _____
○ _____
○ _____
○ _____
○ _____
○ _____

F R I • May 22, 2020

○
○
○
○
○
○
○

S A T • May 23, 2020

○
○
○
○
○
○
○

S U N • May 24, 2020

○
○
○
○
○
○
○

NOTES

TO DO

○
○
○
○
○
○
○

MON • May 25, 2020

○
○
○
○
○
○
○
○

TUE • May 26, 2020

○
○
○
○
○
○
○

WED • May 27, 2020

○
○
○
○
○
○
○

THU • May 28, 2020

○
○
○
○
○
○
○

F R I • May 29, 2020

_____   ○ _____
_____   ○ _____
_____   ○ _____
_____   ○ _____
_____   ○ _____
_____   ○ _____
_____   ○ _____

S A T • May 30, 2020

_____   ○ _____
_____   ○ _____
_____   ○ _____
_____   ○ _____
_____   ○ _____
_____   ○ _____
_____   ○ _____

S U N • May 31, 2020

_____   ○ _____
_____   ○ _____
_____   ○ _____
_____   ○ _____
_____   ○ _____
_____   ○ _____
_____   ○ _____

NOTES

_____
_____
_____
_____
_____

TO DO

○ _____
○ _____
○ _____
○ _____
○ _____
○ _____
○ _____

MON • June 01, 2020

_____ ○ _____
_____ ○ _____
_____ ○ _____
_____ ○ _____
_____ ○ _____
_____ ○ _____
_____ ○ _____
_____ ○ _____

TUE • June 02, 2020

_____ ○ _____
_____ ○ _____
_____ ○ _____
_____ ○ _____
_____ ○ _____
_____ ○ _____
_____ ○ _____

WED • June 03, 2020

_____ ○ _____
_____ ○ _____
_____ ○ _____
_____ ○ _____
_____ ○ _____
_____ ○ _____
_____ ○ _____

THU • June 04, 2020

_____ ○ _____
_____ ○ _____
_____ ○ _____
_____ ○ _____
_____ ○ _____
_____ ○ _____
_____ ○ _____

■ F R I • June 05, 2020

○
○
○
○
○
○
○

■ S A T • June 06, 2020

○
○
○
○
○
○
○

■ S U N • June 07, 2020

○
○
○
○
○
○
○

NOTES

TO DO

○
○
○
○
○
○
○

MON • June 08, 2020

_____ ○
_____ ○ _____
_____ ○ _____
_____ ○ _____
_____ ○ _____
_____ ○ _____
_____ ○ _____
                                  ○

TUE • June 09, 2020

_____ ○
_____ ○ _____
_____ ○ _____
_____ ○ _____
_____ ○ _____
_____ ○ _____
_____ ○ _____
                                  ○

WED • June 10, 2020

_____ ○
_____ ○ _____
_____ ○ _____
_____ ○ _____
_____ ○ _____
_____ ○ _____
_____ ○ _____

THU • June 11, 2020

_____ ○
_____ ○ _____
_____ ○ _____
_____ ○ _____
_____ ○ _____
_____ ○ _____
_____ ○ _____

FRI • June 12, 2020

_____ ○ _____
_____ ○ _____
_____ ○ _____
_____ ○ _____
_____ ○ _____
_____ ○ _____
_____ ○ _____

SAT • June 13, 2020

_____ ○ _____
_____ ○ _____
_____ ○ _____
_____ ○ _____
_____ ○ _____
_____ ○ _____
_____ ○ _____

SUN • June 14, 2020

_____ ○ _____
_____ ○ _____
_____ ○ _____
_____ ○ _____
_____ ○ _____
_____ ○ _____
_____ ○ _____

NOTES

TO DO

_____ ○ _____
_____ ○ _____
_____ ○ _____
_____ ○ _____
_____ ○ _____
_____ ○ _____
                         ○ _____

MON • June 15, 2020

_____
_____   ○   _____
_____   ○   _____
_____   ○   _____
_____   ○   _____
_____   ○   _____
                                   ○   _____
                                   ○   _____

TUE • June 16, 2020

_____   ○   _____
_____   ○   _____
_____   ○   _____
_____   ○   _____
_____   ○   _____
_____   ○   _____
_____   ○   _____

WED • June 17, 2020

_____   ○   _____
_____   ○   _____
_____   ○   _____
_____   ○   _____
_____   ○   _____
_____   ○   _____
_____   ○   _____

THU • June 18, 2020

_____   ○   _____
_____   ○   _____
_____   ○   _____
_____   ○   _____
_____   ○   _____
_____   ○   _____
_____   ○   _____

F R I • June 19, 2020

- _____ ○ _____
- _____ ○ _____
- _____ ○ _____
- _____ ○ _____
- _____ ○ _____
- _____ ○ _____
- _____ ○ _____

S A T • June 20, 2020

- _____ ○ _____
- _____ ○ _____
- _____ ○ _____
- _____ ○ _____
- _____ ○ _____
- _____ ○ _____
- _____ ○ _____

S U N • June 21, 2020

- _____ ○ _____
- _____ ○ _____
- _____ ○ _____
- _____ ○ _____
- _____ ○ _____
- _____ ○ _____
- _____ ○ _____

NOTES

TO DO

- _____ ○ _____
- _____ ○ _____
- _____ ○ _____
- _____ ○ _____
- _____ ○ _____
- _____ ○ _____
- _____ ○ _____

MON • June 22, 2020

_____   ○   _____
_____   ○   _____
_____   ○   _____
_____   ○   _____
_____   ○   _____
_____   ○   _____
_____   ○   _____
_____   ○

TUE • June 23, 2020

_____   ○   _____
_____   ○   _____
_____   ○   _____
_____   ○   _____
_____   ○   _____
_____   ○   _____
_____   ○   _____
_____   ○

WED • June 24, 2020

_____   ○   _____
_____   ○   _____
_____   ○   _____
_____   ○   _____
_____   ○   _____
_____   ○   _____
_____   ○   _____

THU • June 25, 2020

_____   ○   _____
_____   ○   _____
_____   ○   _____
_____   ○   _____
_____   ○   _____
_____   ○   _____
_____   ○

FRI • June 26, 2020

- ○
- ○
- ○
- ○
- ○
- ○
- ○

SAT • June 27, 2020

- ○
- ○
- ○
- ○
- ○
- ○
- ○

SUN • June 28, 2020

- ○
- ○
- ○
- ○
- ○
- ○
- ○

NOTES

TO DO

- ○
- ○
- ○
- ○
- ○
- ○
- ○

MON • June 29, 2020

_____   ○
_____   ○   _____
_____   ○   _____
_____   ○   _____
_____   ○   _____
_____   ○   _____
_____   ○   _____
_____   ○   _____

TUE • June 30, 2020

_____   ○   _____
_____   ○   _____
_____   ○   _____
_____   ○   _____
_____   ○   _____
_____   ○   _____
_____   ○   _____

WED • July 01, 2020

_____   ○   _____
_____   ○   _____
_____   ○   _____
_____   ○   _____
_____   ○   _____
_____   ○   _____
_____   ○   _____

THU • July 02, 2020

_____   ○   _____
_____   ○   _____
_____   ○   _____
_____   ○   _____
_____   ○   _____
_____   ○   _____
_____   ○

F R I • July 03, 2020

_____ ◯ _____
_____ ◯ _____
_____ ◯ _____
_____ ◯ _____
_____ ◯ _____
_____ ◯ _____
_____ ◯ _____

S A T • July 04, 2020

_____ ◯ _____
_____ ◯ _____
_____ ◯ _____
_____ ◯ _____
_____ ◯ _____
_____ ◯ _____
_____ ◯ _____

S U N • July 05, 2020

_____ ◯ _____
_____ ◯ _____
_____ ◯ _____
_____ ◯ _____
_____ ◯ _____
_____ ◯ _____
_____ ◯ _____

NOTES

_____
_____
_____
_____
_____
_____

TO DO

◯ _____
◯ _____
◯ _____
◯ _____
◯ _____
◯ _____
◯ _____

MON • July 06, 2020

_____
_____
_____
_____
_____
_____
_____

○ _____
○ _____
○ _____
○ _____
○ _____
○ _____
○ _____

TUE • July 07, 2020

_____
_____
_____
_____
_____
_____
_____

○ _____
○ _____
○ _____
○ _____
○ _____
○ _____
○ _____

WED • July 08, 2020

_____
_____
_____
_____
_____
_____

○ _____
○ _____
○ _____
○ _____
○ _____
○ _____
○ _____

THU • July 09, 2020

_____
_____
_____
_____
_____
_____

○ _____
○ _____
○ _____
○ _____
○ _____
○ _____
○ _____

■ F R I • July 10, 2020

_____ ○ _____
_____ ○ _____
_____ ○ _____
_____ ○ _____
_____ ○ _____
_____ ○ _____
_____ ○ _____

■ S A T • July 11, 2020

_____ ○ _____
_____ ○ _____
_____ ○ _____
_____ ○ _____
_____ ○ _____
_____ ○ _____
_____ ○ _____

■ S U N • July 12, 2020

_____ ○ _____
_____ ○ _____
_____ ○ _____
_____ ○ _____
_____ ○ _____
_____ ○ _____
_____ ○ _____

NOTES   ## TO DO

_____ ○ _____
_____ ○ _____
_____ ○ _____
_____ ○ _____
_____ ○ _____
_____ ○ _____
                          ○ _____

MON • July 13, 2020

_____   ○   _____
_____   ○   _____
_____   ○   _____
_____   ○   _____
_____   ○   _____
_____   ○   _____
_____   ○   _____
_____   ○   _____

TUE • July 14, 2020

_____   ○   _____
_____   ○   _____
_____   ○   _____
_____   ○   _____
_____   ○   _____
_____   ○   _____
_____   ○   _____

WED • July 15, 2020

_____   ○   _____
_____   ○   _____
_____   ○   _____
_____   ○   _____
_____   ○   _____
_____   ○   _____
_____   ○   _____

THU • July 16, 2020

_____   ○   _____
_____   ○   _____
_____   ○   _____
_____   ○   _____
_____   ○   _____
_____   ○   _____
_____   ○   _____

■ F R I • July 17, 2020

_____ ○ _____
_____ ○ _____
_____ ○ _____
_____ ○ _____
_____ ○ _____
_____ ○ _____
_____ ○ _____

■ S A T • July 18, 2020

_____ ○ _____
_____ ○ _____
_____ ○ _____
_____ ○ _____
_____ ○ _____
_____ ○ _____
_____ ○ _____

■ S U N • July 19, 2020

_____ ○ _____
_____ ○ _____
_____ ○ _____
_____ ○ _____
_____ ○ _____
_____ ○ _____
_____ ○ _____

NOTES

_____
_____
_____
_____
_____
_____

TO DO

○ _____
○ _____
○ _____
○ _____
○ _____
○ _____
○ _____

MON • July 20, 2020

_____ ◯
_____ ◯ _____
_____ ◯ _____
_____ ◯ _____
_____ ◯ _____
_____ ◯ _____
_____ ◯ _____
                         ◯ _____

TUE • July 21, 2020

_____ ◯
_____ ◯ _____
_____ ◯ _____
_____ ◯ _____
_____ ◯ _____
_____ ◯ _____
_____ ◯ _____
                         ◯ _____

WED • July 22, 2020

_____ ◯
_____ ◯ _____
_____ ◯ _____
_____ ◯ _____
_____ ◯ _____
_____ ◯ _____
_____ ◯ _____
                         ◯ _____

THU • July 23, 2020

_____ ◯
_____ ◯ _____
_____ ◯ _____
_____ ◯ _____
_____ ◯ _____
_____ ◯ _____
_____ ◯ _____
                         ◯ _____

F R I • July 24, 2020

○
○
○
○
○
○
○

S A T • July 25, 2020

○
○
○
○
○
○
○

S U N • July 26, 2020

○
○
○
○
○
○
○

NOTES

TO DO

○
○
○
○
○
○
○

MON • July 27, 2020

○
○
○
○
○
○
○

TUE • July 28, 2020

○
○
○
○
○
○
○

WED • July 29, 2020

○
○
○
○
○
○
○

THU • July 30, 2020

○
○
○
○
○
○
○

■ F R I • July 31, 2020

_____   ○ _____
_____   ○ _____
_____   ○ _____
_____   ○ _____
_____   ○ _____
_____   ○ _____
_____   ○ _____

■ S A T • August 01, 2020

_____   ○ _____
_____   ○ _____
_____   ○ _____
_____   ○ _____
_____   ○ _____
_____   ○ _____
_____   ○ _____

■ S U N • August 02, 2020

_____   ○ _____
_____   ○ _____
_____   ○ _____
_____   ○ _____
_____   ○ _____
_____   ○ _____
_____   ○ _____

NOTES   ## TO DO

_____   ○ _____
_____   ○ _____
_____   ○ _____
_____   ○ _____
_____   ○ _____
_____   ○ _____
_____   ○ _____

M O N • August 03, 2020

○
○
○
○
○
○
○

T U E • August 04, 2020

○
○
○
○
○
○
○

W E D • August 05, 2020

○
○
○
○
○
○
○

T H U • August 06, 2020

○
○
○
○
○
○
○

■ F R I • August 07, 2020

_____   ○ _____
_____   ○ _____
_____   ○ _____
_____   ○ _____
_____   ○ _____
_____   ○ _____
_____   ○ _____

■ S A T • August 08, 2020

_____   ○ _____
_____   ○ _____
_____   ○ _____
_____   ○ _____
_____   ○ _____
_____   ○ _____
_____   ○ _____

■ S U N • August 09, 2020

_____   ○ _____
_____   ○ _____
_____   ○ _____
_____   ○ _____
_____   ○ _____
_____   ○ _____
_____   ○ _____

NOTES   TO DO

_____   ○ _____
_____   ○ _____
_____   ○ _____
_____   ○ _____
_____   ○ _____
_____   ○ _____
_____   ○ _____

◼ M O N • August 10, 2020

_____ ○ _____
_____ ○ _____
_____ ○ _____
_____ ○ _____
_____ ○ _____
_____ ○ _____
_____ ○ _____

◼ T U E • August 11, 2020

_____ ○ _____
_____ ○ _____
_____ ○ _____
_____ ○ _____
_____ ○ _____
_____ ○ _____
_____ ○ _____

◼ W E D • August 12, 2020

_____ ○ _____
_____ ○ _____
_____ ○ _____
_____ ○ _____
_____ ○ _____
_____ ○ _____
_____ ○ _____

◼ T H U • August 13, 2020

_____ ○ _____
_____ ○ _____
_____ ○ _____
_____ ○ _____
_____ ○ _____
_____ ○ _____
_____ ○ _____

F R I • August 14, 2020

○
○
○
○
○
○
○

S A T • August 15, 2020

○
○
○
○
○
○
○

S U N • August 16, 2020

○
○
○
○
○
○
○

NOTES

TO DO

○
○
○
○
○
○
○

MON • August 17, 2020

○
○
○
○
○
○
○

TUE • August 18, 2020

○
○
○
○
○
○
○

WED • August 19, 2020

○
○
○
○
○
○
○

THU • August 20, 2020

○
○
○
○
○
○
○

◼ F R I • August 21, 2020

_____   ○ _____
_____   ○ _____
_____   ○ _____
_____   ○ _____
_____   ○ _____
_____   ○ _____
_____   ○ _____

◼ S A T • August 22, 2020

_____   ○ _____
_____   ○ _____
_____   ○ _____
_____   ○ _____
_____   ○ _____
_____   ○ _____
_____   ○ _____

◼ S U N • August 23, 2020

_____   ○ _____
_____   ○ _____
_____   ○ _____
_____   ○ _____
_____   ○ _____
_____   ○ _____
_____   ○ _____

NOTES   # TO DO

_____   ○ _____
_____   ○ _____
_____   ○ _____
_____   ○ _____
_____   ○ _____
_____   ○ _____
_____   ○ _____

MON • August 24, 2020

- ◯
- ◯
- ◯
- ◯
- ◯
- ◯
- ◯

TUE • August 25, 2020

- ◯
- ◯
- ◯
- ◯
- ◯
- ◯
- ◯

WED • August 26, 2020

- ◯
- ◯
- ◯
- ◯
- ◯
- ◯
- ◯

THU • August 27, 2020

- ◯
- ◯
- ◯
- ◯
- ◯
- ◯
- ◯

F R I • August 28, 2020

_____ ○ _____
_____ ○ _____
_____ ○ _____
_____ ○ _____
_____ ○ _____
_____ ○ _____
_____ ○ _____

S A T • August 29, 2020

_____ ○ _____
_____ ○ _____
_____ ○ _____
_____ ○ _____
_____ ○ _____
_____ ○ _____
_____ ○ _____

S U N • August 30, 2020

_____ ○ _____
_____ ○ _____
_____ ○ _____
_____ ○ _____
_____ ○ _____
_____ ○ _____
_____ ○ _____

NOTES   TO DO

_____ ○ _____
_____ ○ _____
_____ ○ _____
_____ ○ _____
_____ ○ _____
_____ ○ _____
_____ ○ _____

MON • August 31, 2020

_____ ○ _____
_____ ○ _____
_____ ○ _____
_____ ○ _____
_____ ○ _____
_____ ○ _____
_____ ○ _____

TUE • September 01, 2020

_____ ○ _____
_____ ○ _____
_____ ○ _____
_____ ○ _____
_____ ○ _____
_____ ○ _____
_____ ○ _____

WED • September 02, 2020

_____ ○ _____
_____ ○ _____
_____ ○ _____
_____ ○ _____
_____ ○ _____
_____ ○ _____
_____ ○ _____

THU • September 03, 2020

_____ ○ _____
_____ ○ _____
_____ ○ _____
_____ ○ _____
_____ ○ _____
_____ ○ _____
_____ ○ _____

■ F R I • September 04, 2020

_____
_____   ○ _____
_____   ○ _____
_____   ○ _____
_____   ○ _____
_____   ○ _____
_____   ○ _____
                                     ○ _____

■ S A T • September 05, 2020

_____
_____   ○ _____
_____   ○ _____
_____   ○ _____
_____   ○ _____
_____   ○ _____
_____   ○ _____
                                     ○ _____

■ S U N • September 06, 2020

_____
_____   ○ _____
_____   ○ _____
_____   ○ _____
_____   ○ _____
_____   ○ _____
_____   ○ _____
                                     ○ _____

NOTES   ## TO DO

_____   ○ _____
_____   ○ _____
_____   ○ _____
_____   ○ _____
_____   ○ _____
_____   ○ _____
                                     ○ _____

MON • September 07, 2020

○
○
○
○
○
○
○

TUE • September 08, 2020

○
○
○
○
○
○
○

WED • September 09, 2020

○
○
○
○
○
○
○

THU • September 10, 2020

○
○
○
○
○
○
○

F R I • September 11, 2020

_____ ○ _____
_____ ○ _____
_____ ○ _____
_____ ○ _____
_____ ○ _____
_____ ○ _____
_____ ○ _____

S A T • September 12, 2020

_____ ○ _____
_____ ○ _____
_____ ○ _____
_____ ○ _____
_____ ○ _____
_____ ○ _____
_____ ○ _____

S U N • September 13, 2020

_____ ○ _____
_____ ○ _____
_____ ○ _____
_____ ○ _____
_____ ○ _____
_____ ○ _____
_____ ○ _____

NOTES   ## TO DO

_____ ○ _____
_____ ○ _____
_____ ○ _____
_____ ○ _____
_____ ○ _____
_____ ○ _____
_____ ○ _____

MON • September 14, 2020

○
○
○
○
○
○
○

TUE • September 15, 2020

○
○
○
○
○
○
○

WED • September 16, 2020

○
○
○
○
○
○
○

THU • September 17, 2020

○
○
○
○
○
○
○

FRI • September 18, 2020

_____ ○ _____
_____ ○ _____
_____ ○ _____
_____ ○ _____
_____ ○ _____
_____ ○ _____
_____ ○ _____

SAT • September 19, 2020

_____ ○ _____
_____ ○ _____
_____ ○ _____
_____ ○ _____
_____ ○ _____
_____ ○ _____
_____ ○ _____

SUN • September 20, 2020

_____ ○ _____
_____ ○ _____
_____ ○ _____
_____ ○ _____
_____ ○ _____
_____ ○ _____
_____ ○ _____

NOTES

_____

_____

_____

_____

_____

TO DO

○ _____
○ _____
○ _____
○ _____
○ _____
○ _____
○ _____

MON • September 21, 2020

○
○
○
○
○
○
○

TUE • September 22, 2020

○
○
○
○
○
○
○

WED • September 23, 2020

○
○
○
○
○
○
○

THU • September 24, 2020

○
○
○
○
○
○
○

F R I • September 25, 2020

_____ ○ _____
_____ ○ _____
_____ ○ _____
_____ ○ _____
_____ ○ _____
_____ ○ _____
_____ ○ _____

S A T • September 26, 2020

_____ ○ _____
_____ ○ _____
_____ ○ _____
_____ ○ _____
_____ ○ _____
_____ ○ _____
_____ ○ _____

S U N • September 27, 2020

_____ ○ _____
_____ ○ _____
_____ ○ _____
_____ ○ _____
_____ ○ _____
_____ ○ _____
_____ ○ _____

NOTES

_____
_____
_____
_____
_____
_____

TO DO

○ _____
○ _____
○ _____
○ _____
○ _____
○ _____
○ _____

MON • September 28, 2020

○
○
○
○
○
○
○

TUE • September 29, 2020

○
○
○
○
○
○
○

WED • September 30, 2020

○
○
○
○
○
○
○

THU • October 01, 2020

○
○
○
○
○
○
○

■ F R I • October 02, 2020

_____ ○ _____
_____ ○ _____
_____ ○ _____
_____ ○ _____
_____ ○ _____
_____ ○ _____
_____ ○ _____

■ S A T • October 03, 2020

_____ ○ _____
_____ ○ _____
_____ ○ _____
_____ ○ _____
_____ ○ _____
_____ ○ _____
_____ ○ _____

■ S U N • October 04, 2020

_____ ○ _____
_____ ○ _____
_____ ○ _____
_____ ○ _____
_____ ○ _____
_____ ○ _____
_____ ○ _____

NOTES

_____

_____

_____

_____

_____

_____

TO DO

○ _____
○ _____
○ _____
○ _____
○ _____
○ _____
○ _____

MON • October 05, 2020

_____   ○ _____
_____   ○ _____
_____   ○ _____
_____   ○ _____
_____   ○ _____
_____   ○ _____
_____   ○ _____

TUE • October 06, 2020

_____   ○ _____
_____   ○ _____
_____   ○ _____
_____   ○ _____
_____   ○ _____
_____   ○ _____
_____   ○ _____

WED • October 07, 2020

_____   ○ _____
_____   ○ _____
_____   ○ _____
_____   ○ _____
_____   ○ _____
_____   ○ _____
_____   ○ _____

THU • October 08, 2020

_____   ○ _____
_____   ○ _____
_____   ○ _____
_____   ○ _____
_____   ○ _____
_____   ○ _____
_____   ○ _____

F R I • October 09, 2020

S A T • October 10, 2020

S U N • October 11, 2020

NOTES

TO DO

M O N • October 12, 2020

_____ ○
_____ ○ _____
_____ ○ _____
_____ ○ _____
_____ ○ _____
_____ ○ _____
_____ ○ _____
_____ ○ _____

T U E • October 13, 2020

_____ ○
_____ ○ _____
_____ ○ _____
_____ ○ _____
_____ ○ _____
_____ ○ _____
_____ ○ _____
_____ ○ _____

W E D • October 14, 2020

_____ ○
_____ ○ _____
_____ ○ _____
_____ ○ _____
_____ ○ _____
_____ ○ _____
_____ ○ _____
_____ ○ _____

T H U • October 15, 2020

_____ ○
_____ ○ _____
_____ ○ _____
_____ ○ _____
_____ ○ _____
_____ ○ _____
_____ ○ _____
_____ ○ _____

◼ F R I • October 16, 2020

_____   ○ _____
_____   ○ _____
_____   ○ _____
_____   ○ _____
_____   ○ _____
_____   ○ _____
_____   ○ _____

◼ S A T • October 17, 2020

_____   ○ _____
_____   ○ _____
_____   ○ _____
_____   ○ _____
_____   ○ _____
_____   ○ _____
_____   ○ _____

◼ S U N • October 18, 2020

_____   ○ _____
_____   ○ _____
_____   ○ _____
_____   ○ _____
_____   ○ _____
_____   ○ _____
_____   ○ _____

NOTES   ## TO DO

_____   ○ _____
_____   ○ _____
_____   ○ _____
_____   ○ _____
_____   ○ _____
_____   ○ _____
_____   ○ _____

MON • October 19, 2020

○
○
○
○
○
○
○

TUE • October 20, 2020

○
○
○
○
○
○
○

WED • October 21, 2020

○
○
○
○
○
○
○

THU • October 22, 2020

○
○
○
○
○
○
○

FRI • October 23, 2020

_____ ○ _____
_____ ○ _____
_____ ○ _____
_____ ○ _____
_____ ○ _____
_____ ○ _____
_____ ○ _____

SAT • October 24, 2020

_____ ○ _____
_____ ○ _____
_____ ○ _____
_____ ○ _____
_____ ○ _____
_____ ○ _____
_____ ○ _____

SUN • October 25, 2020

_____ ○ _____
_____ ○ _____
_____ ○ _____
_____ ○ _____
_____ ○ _____
_____ ○ _____
_____ ○ _____

NOTES   ## TO DO

_____ ○ _____
_____ ○ _____
_____ ○ _____
_____ ○ _____
_____ ○ _____
_____ ○ _____
_____ ○ _____

MON • October 26, 2020

_____
_____
_____
_____
_____
_____
_____

○ _____
○ _____
○ _____
○ _____
○ _____
○ _____
○ _____

TUE • October 27, 2020

_____
_____
_____
_____
_____
_____
_____

○ _____
○ _____
○ _____
○ _____
○ _____
○ _____
○ _____

WED • October 28, 2020

_____
_____
_____
_____
_____
_____
_____

○ _____
○ _____
○ _____
○ _____
○ _____
○ _____
○ _____

THU • October 29, 2020

_____
_____
_____
_____
_____
_____
_____

○ _____
○ _____
○ _____
○ _____
○ _____
○ _____
○ _____

◼ F R I • October 30, 2020

○
○
○
○
○
○
○

◼ S A T • October 31, 2020

○
○
○
○
○
○
○

◼ S U N • November 01, 2020

○
○
○
○
○
○
○

NOTES

TO DO

○
○
○
○
○
○
○

MON • November 02, 2020

○
○
○
○
○
○
○
○

TUE • November 03, 2020

○
○
○
○
○
○
○

WED • November 04, 2020

○
○
○
○
○
○
○

THU • November 05, 2020

○
○
○
○
○
○
○

FRI • November 06, 2020

SAT • November 07, 2020

SUN • November 08, 2020

NOTES

TO DO

MON • November 09, 2020

○
○
○
○
○
○
○

TUE • November 10, 2020

○
○
○
○
○
○
○

WED • November 11, 2020

○
○
○
○
○
○
○

THU • November 12, 2020

○
○
○
○
○
○
○

FRI • November 13, 2020

○
○
○
○
○
○
○

SAT • November 14, 2020

○
○
○
○
○
○
○

SUN • November 15, 2020

○
○
○
○
○
○
○

NOTES

TO DO

○
○
○
○
○
○
○

MON • November 16, 2020

○
○
○
○
○
○
○
○

TUE • November 17, 2020

○
○
○
○
○
○
○

WED • November 18, 2020

○
○
○
○
○
○
○

THU • November 19, 2020

○
○
○
○
○
○
○

■ F R I • November 20, 2020

○
○
○
○
○
○
○

■ S A T • November 21, 2020

○
○
○
○
○
○
○

■ S U N • November 22, 2020

○
○
○
○
○
○
○

NOTES

TO DO

○
○
○
○
○
○
○

◼ MON • November 23, 2020

_____ ○ _____
_____ ○ _____
_____ ○ _____
_____ ○ _____
_____ ○ _____
_____ ○ _____
_____ ○ _____

◼ TUE • November 24, 2020

_____ ○ _____
_____ ○ _____
_____ ○ _____
_____ ○ _____
_____ ○ _____
_____ ○ _____
_____ ○ _____

◼ WED • November 25, 2020

_____ ○ _____
_____ ○ _____
_____ ○ _____
_____ ○ _____
_____ ○ _____
_____ ○ _____
_____ ○ _____

◼ THU • November 26, 2020

_____ ○ _____
_____ ○ _____
_____ ○ _____
_____ ○ _____
_____ ○ _____
_____ ○ _____
_____ ○ _____

■ F R I • November 27, 2020

_____   ○ _____
_____   ○ _____
_____   ○ _____
_____   ○ _____
_____   ○ _____
_____   ○ _____
_____   ○ _____

■ S A T • November 28, 2020

_____   ○ _____
_____   ○ _____
_____   ○ _____
_____   ○ _____
_____   ○ _____
_____   ○ _____
_____   ○ _____

■ S U N • November 29, 2020

_____   ○ _____
_____   ○ _____
_____   ○ _____
_____   ○ _____
_____   ○ _____
_____   ○ _____
_____   ○ _____

NOTES   ## TO DO

_____   ○
_____   ○ _____
_____   ○ _____
_____   ○ _____
_____   ○ _____
_____   ○ _____
_____   ○ _____

MON • November 30, 2020

_____
_____
_____
_____
_____
_____
_____

○ _____
○ _____
○ _____
○ _____
○ _____
○ _____
○ _____

TUE • December 01, 2020

_____
_____
_____
_____
_____
_____
_____
_____

○ _____
○ _____
○ _____
○ _____
○ _____
○ _____
○ _____

WED • December 02, 2020

_____
_____
_____
_____
_____
_____
_____

○ _____
○ _____
○ _____
○ _____
○ _____
○ _____
○ _____

THU • December 03, 2020

_____
_____
_____
_____
_____
_____
_____

○ _____
○ _____
○ _____
○ _____
○ _____
○ _____
○ _____

■ F R I • December 04, 2020

○
○
○
○
○
○
○

■ S A T • December 05, 2020

○
○
○
○
○
○
○

■ S U N • December 06, 2020

○
○
○
○
○
○
○

NOTES

TO DO

○
○
○
○
○
○
○

MON • December 07, 2020

_____   ○   _____
_____   ○   _____
_____   ○   _____
_____   ○   _____
_____   ○   _____
_____   ○   _____
_____   ○   _____

TUE • December 08, 2020

_____   ○   _____
_____   ○   _____
_____   ○   _____
_____   ○   _____
_____   ○   _____
_____   ○   _____
_____   ○   _____

WED • December 09, 2020

_____   ○   _____
_____   ○   _____
_____   ○   _____
_____   ○   _____
_____   ○   _____
_____   ○   _____
_____   ○   _____

THU • December 10, 2020

_____   ○   _____
_____   ○   _____
_____   ○   _____
_____   ○   _____
_____   ○   _____
_____   ○   _____
_____   ○   _____

■ F R I • December 11, 2020

_____ ○ _____
_____ ○ _____
_____ ○ _____
_____ ○ _____
_____ ○ _____
_____ ○ _____
_____ ○ _____

■ S A T • December 12, 2020

_____ ○ _____
_____ ○ _____
_____ ○ _____
_____ ○ _____
_____ ○ _____
_____ ○ _____
_____ ○ _____

■ S U N • December 13, 2020

_____ ○ _____
_____ ○ _____
_____ ○ _____
_____ ○ _____
_____ ○ _____
_____ ○ _____
_____ ○ _____

NOTES   ## TO DO

_____ ○ _____
_____ ○ _____
_____ ○ _____
_____ ○ _____
_____ ○ _____
_____ ○ _____
                          ○ _____

M O N • December 14, 2020

T U E • December 15, 2020

W E D • December 16, 2020

T H U • December 17, 2020

FRI • December 18, 2020

○
○
○
○
○
○
○

SAT • December 19, 2020

○
○
○
○
○
○
○

SUN • December 20, 2020

○
○
○
○
○
○
○

NOTES

TO DO

○
○
○
○
○
○
○

MON • December 21, 2020

TUE • December 22, 2020

WED • December 23, 2020

THU • December 24, 2020

FRI • December 25, 2020

○
○
○
○
○
○
○

SAT • December 26, 2020

○
○
○
○
○
○
○

SUN • December 27, 2020

○
○
○
○
○
○
○

NOTES

TO DO

○
○
○
○
○
○
○

M O N • December 28, 2020

T U E • December 29, 2020

W E D • December 30, 2020

T H U • December 31, 2020

Made in the USA
San Bernardino, CA
25 November 2019

60424969R00078